CIRCLE MIRROR TRANSFORMATION

BY **ANNIE BAKER**

D1269623

★

★

DRAMATISTS
PLAY SERVICE
INC.

*This play is dedicated to
Reed Birney, Tracee Chimo, Peter Friedman,
Sam Gold, Didi O'Connell, and Heidi Schreck.*

ACKNOWLEDGMENTS

I would like to thank Adam Greenfield, Tim Sanford, and the entire staff at Playwrights Horizons. You renewed my faith in non-profit theater.

I would also like to thank the following people for their drama-turgical and/or emotional support: Janice Paran, Christopher Hibma, Philip Himberg, Jim Nicola, Linda Chapman, Chris Till, and Michael Chernus.

Finally, I would like to acknowledge the innumerable contributions of my wonderful director and five beautiful actors, to whom this play is dedicated. You improvised and hooped and told your stories and walked around blindfolded and exploded and free-associated and gave yourselves wholeheartedly over to this bizarre little play. Watching you work together made me finally understand what the hell Marty is talking about during that counting exercise.

AUTHOR'S NOTE

Please heed the pauses and the silences in this play. They are of extreme importance — they are just as important as the dialogue — and every one of them was placed in the script with great care. If you skip over or rush through these silences, you are performing a different play.

There will be a point in the rehearsal process when it seems like these pauses and silences are slowing the play down. The actors will worry that the play is boring — that they'll lose the audience's attention — that what they need to do is PICK UP THE PACE.

All I can say is, this is an inevitable feeling and you must fight against it.

Without its silences, this play is a satire, and with its silences it is, hopefully, a strange little naturalistic meditation on theater and life and death and the passing of time.

And by "pause" I do not mean a beat, or a quick gulp of air. A "pause" should be approximately two seconds long ("one mississippi, two mississippi"), a "long pause" should be approximately four seconds long, a "short pause" should be approximately one second long, a "silence" should be approximately five seconds long, and a "long silence" should be at least seven seconds long.

Okay.

I hope that you will portray these characters with compassion. They are not fools. And if you ask me, I think Marty's a great teacher.

CIRCLE MIRROR TRANSFORMATION received its World Premiere at Playwrights Horizons in New York City on October 13, 2009. It was directed by Sam Gold; the set and costume design were by David Zinn; the lighting design was by Mark Barton; the sound design was by Leah Gelpe; and the production stage manager was Alaina Taylor. The cast was as follows:

SCHULTZ .... Reed Birney
JAMES .... Peter Friedman
MARTY .... Deirdre O'Connell
LAUREN .... Tracee Chimo
THERESA .... Heidi Schreck

CHARACTERS

MARTY, 55

JAMES, 60

SCHULTZ, 48

THERESA, 35

LAUREN, 16

PLACE

A windowless dance studio in the town of Shirley, Vermont.
There is a wall of mirrors. There is a big blue yoga ball.

TIME

Summertime.

Note: The week titles (WEEK ONE, WEEK TWO, etc.) should somehow be projected and/or displayed onstage but not the scene numbers (I, II, etc.).

A forward slash ("/") indicates overlapping dialogue.

CIRCLE MIRROR TRANSFORMATION

PROLOGUE

Lights up. Marty, James, Theresa, Lauren, and Schultz are all lying on the floor, in various positions. After at least fifteen seconds of silence:

THERESA. One.

(A long silence.)

JAMES. Two.

(Silence.)

LAUREN and SCHULTZ. Three.
MARTY. Start again.

(Silence.)

SCHULTZ. One.
MARTY. Two.
JAMES. Three.

(Another long silence.)

LAUREN. Four.
MARTY. ... Five.
JAMES. Six.

(Silence.)

THERESA and SCHULTZ. Seven.
SCHULTZ. Shoot.
MARTY. Start again.

(Silence.)

SCHULTZ and JAMES. One.
LAUREN. … Oh my god.
MARTY. Okay. Wait.
> We're not getting it.
> *(Pause.)*
> Let's all …   everyone take a deep breath.
> *(Pause.)*
> Okay.

(About five seconds go by.)

JAMES. One.

(Silence.)

THERESA and LAUREN. Two.
MARTY. Start again.

(Blackout.)

WEEK ONE

I

James is standing center stage, facing the audience. The rest of the class sits downstage, facing James.

JAMES. Hi.

My name is Marty Kreisberg. Short for Martha, but they've been calling me Marty since I was born.

Ah ...

(He scratches his head, then grins.)

My husband is supposed to do this, ah, monologue about me but he doesn't really know what to —

(Marty is trying to signal something to him.)

Why can't I do that?

(He shakes his head.)

Allrightallright.

I'm 55 and I'm, ah ... I live in Shirley, Vermont. I'm co-executive director here at the Community Center and I also teach a bunch of classes ... ah ... pottery, jewelry making, creative drama for youth ... I've been pushing for an adult creative drama class for a while and I'm ... I'm really glad they let me do it.

(Pause.)

Okay.

Ah ... I'm from New Jersey. Originally. I don't have any kids, but I'm a great stepmother.

My husband is named James. He's in the class, too.

Ah ... let's see. I'm really into nontraditional healing and sort of ... unconventional, ah ...

(He scratches his head again.)

I'm 55 years old. I really love the Southwest. I hope to move there someday.

Did I already say that?

Okay.

(Blackout.)

II

Theresa, Schultz, Lauren, and James are walking around the room in different directions, sock-footed. This should last at least 30 seconds. Everyone is taking this seriously. Marty is sitting on her yoga ball, watching.

MARTY. … Faster.

(They all walk a little faster, still going in different directions.)

MARTY. … Even faster.

(They start zooming around the room, except for Lauren, who tries to keep a safe distance away from everyone.)

MARTY. Now … I want you to slow down.
  (Pause.)
Start noticing everyone around you.

(They all keep walking while making an effort to notice everyone around them. About 20 seconds pass.)

MARTY. … And I want you to find people and shake their hand.

(They obey. 20 more seconds pass.)

MARTY. Now say your name when you shake hands!

(About 30 seconds of walking/shaking hands/saying your own name.)

MARTY. Okay! Good.

Great.
Stop.

(They stop and look at her. She smiles at them.)

MARTY. How'd that feel?

(An awkward silence.)

THERESA.	SCHULTZ.
Great.	Weird.
	… Good.

MARTY. Okay.
  (She gets up off her ball.)
  Um.
  Well.
  Welcome.
  (Pause.)
  I just … I'm so excited to get to know all of you.
  (An even longer pause.)
  I um … I don't want to talk too much, because that's …
  (She makes a vague gesture with her hands.)
  But. Um. I just hope that you all feel, um, safe here. And open.
  And willing to *go* with it.
  Ah … okay.
  Let's keep going!

(Blackout.)

III

Marty, Theresa, Lauren, James, and Schultz are sitting in a circle.

MARTY. I
THERESA. Took
LAUREN. This
JAMES. Class
SCHULTZ. Because
MARTY. It
THERESA. Was
LAUREN. In
JAMES. The
SCHULTZ. ... Paper.

(A weird pause.)

MARTY. Love
THERESA. ... Truth!
LAUREN. Um ... discovery
JAMES. Self-actualization
SCHULTZ. ... Friends
MARTY. Were
THERESA. Part
LAUREN. Of
JAMES. All
SCHULTZ. The
MARTY. Mess!
THERESA. And
LAUREN. *(Pause.)*
    Stuff.
JAMES. ... Enormous.

(A confused pause.)

SCHULTZ. I
MARTY. Feel
THERESA. Fantastic!
LAUREN. Period.
MARTY. Oh. Hey. Yeah. I forgot to — we don't have to ... you don't have to say "period." You can just / keep —
JAMES. Pain
SCHULTZ. Um ... ah ... Loneliness
MARTY. Are
THERESA. Feeding
LAUREN. Me
JAMES. ... Sky.

(Pause.)

SCHULTZ. Evil
MARTY. ... Blue
THERESA. Birds
LAUREN. Fly
JAMES. Over
SCHULTZ. Head.

(Pause.)

MARTY. Green
THERESA. Wondrous
LAUREN. Um ... Sunshine
JAMES. Washes
SCHULTZ. Over
MARTY. My
THERESA. Little
LAUREN. Tiny
JAMES. Face

(Pause.)

SCHULTZ. ... Hopefully.

(Pause.)

MARTY. Okay.
    Great.
    (Pause.)
    Maybe next week we'll try to make it a little more like a real story.

(Blackout.)

IV

Breaktime.

Schultz and Theresa are the only people in the room. Theresa is squatting in the corner, listening to a cell phone message. Schultz is drinking from a bottle of water and eyeing her.

SCHULTZ. How long did she say?

(Theresa holds up one finger and mouths "Sorry." After a few seconds she snaps her phone shut.)

THERESA. Sorry. What?
SCHULTZ. How long did she …
    (A pause while he tries to reformulate his thoughts.)
    Ah …
    How long is the break?
THERESA. I think she said ten minutes?

(Schultz nods, embarrassed, and goes back to drinking water. Theresa watches him drink and smiles at him. He puts down the water and smiles back at her.)

SCHULTZ. I'm sorry. You have …
    Sorry.
    Do you / ah —

THERESA. What?

SCHULTZ. I just ah …

    I was going to say that you have very … you have very alive *eyes*.

THERESA. Oh. Wow. I —

SCHULTZ. But that sounds / kind of —

THERESA. No! Thank you.

SCHULTZ. I don't mean it in a, uh … in a weird way.

THERESA. No. It's a — it's a compliment.

(They smile at each other. A pause.)

SCHULTZ. What's your deal?

THERESA. Oh. God. I / um —

SCHULTZ. I just mean … I haven't seen you around. It's a small town, / so —

THERESA. I moved here like five months ago.

SCHULTZ. All right.

(A pause.)

THERESA. Do you live near here? Or do / you —

SCHULTZ. I live in the Brook.

THERESA. I'm … what? Sorry. / The —

SCHULTZ. They're condos. The Brook. It's on Hitchcock? Right off 7. Across from / the —

THERESA. Oh yeah. I know where that is.

(A silence, during which Theresa notices his wedding ring.)

THERESA. So do you live there alone or do / you —

SCHULTZ. I live there alone.

    (Pause.)

    My wife and I recently … we're divorced. That's why I live in the, uh … I moved out about a year ago.

THERESA. Oh. Okay.

SCHULTZ. She lives in our house. It's a great house. With a … I spent years working on the garden.

THERESA. Huh.

SCHULTZ. The Brook is … it's very corporate. Very corporate-feeling.

(Theresa smiles sympathetically at him. Another silence.)

THERESA. I was just confused because you um … you're still wearing your wedding ring.

(Schultz looks down at his hand.)

SCHULTZ. Yes. Yes I am.

(Lauren enters, her cell phone pressed to her ear. She eyes them suspiciously, then goes over to her bag, rummages through it, removes something, slips it into her pocket, and then leaves. They watch her.)

SCHULTZ. I should probably take it off.
THERESA. Yeah. I don't know. What's the rush, I guess.

(Pause.)

SCHULTZ. Would you be interested / in —

(Marty and James enter, in the middle of talking.)

JAMES. So *she* called *you.*
MARTY. Yeah. We / just —
JAMES. What'd you talk about?
MARTY. Nothing really.
   (She looks up and smiles at Theresa and James.)
We've got about three more minutes, you guys.

(James walks out of the room. A weird silence. Marty's cell phone rings. She takes it out and looks at it, then puts it back in her pocket.)

SCHULTZ. *(To Theresa.)*
   So you're a … you like to hula hoop!
THERESA. Um. The correct term is actually "hooping."
SCHULTZ. Oh god. I'm sorry.
THERESA. No, no. It's a common, um … but "hula hooping" is, actually, um … it's a misnaming.
SCHULTZ. Ah.

(Schultz keeps staring at the hoop. James reenters and stands near the doorway, watching Schultz and Theresa.)

SCHULTZ. It's big.
THERESA. The big ones are actually easier to use.
    Wanna see?
MARTY. We're about to start. Whenever Lauren gets back.
THERESA. It'll take two seconds.

(Theresa runs over to the corner, gets the hoop, and runs back to the center of the room. Schultz stands aside while she raises the hoop to her hips and then, with a few small, deft tilts of her pelvis, begins hooping.)

SCHULTZ. … Wow.

(Theresa continues hooping. After a while:)

THERESA. The key is actually less movement.
SCHULTZ. Uh-huh.
THERESA. As opposed to more movement.

(Now Marty and James are watching, too. Everyone is a little hypnotized.)

SCHULTZ. Jesus.

(Theresa stops and gracefully catches the hoop before it falls to the ground.)

THERESA. *(To Schultz.)*
    Try it.
SCHULTZ. Oh. No. I can't. / I ah —
THERESA. It's actually really easy.

(Schultz shakes his head.)

THERESA. Schultz.
SCHULTZ. Nope.

(Lauren reenters, turning off her cell phone.)

MARTY. Oop! You know what? Everyone's back. Let's get / started.
JAMES. *(Suddenly.)*
    I'll try it.
THERESA. Yeah James!

(James walks over to Theresa. She hands him the hoop, and he steps into it.)

JAMES. What do I do?
THERESA. Okay. Just um … put one foot forward.

(James puts one foot forward.)

JAMES. Uh-huh.
THERESA. Now just … try it. Don't think too much.

(James throws his pelvis forward and sends the hoop aloft. It crashes to the ground in about three seconds.)

JAMES. *(Shaking his head.)*
    Ah.
THERESA. Try again. It's just a little motion. Like a little … spin.

(James tries again. He sends the hoop aloft, awkwardly swinging his hips back and forth.)

THERESA. Good! Oh my god! That's awesome!

(Everyone watches James, half-impressed, half-aghast. The hoop crashes to the ground. Schultz and Theresa and Lauren all applaud. James hands the hoop back to Theresa.)

MARTY. That was amazing.

(Blackout.)

V

Lights up. They are all sitting in a circle. Marty is in the middle of a story. Everyone is rapt.

MARTY. And it was at this ... this wedding was like ... it was a real hippie wedding. We were all sleeping on the floor of ... we were sleeping in the lobby of this old abandoned hotel in Eureka. And I spread out my little straw mat ... this was at the end of the night, and we were all a little drunk, and we'd been dancing, and singing, and I was about to go to sleep, but then I looked over ... and next to me, lying on his little straw mat, was this, um, this *guy.*

(Pause.)

This really cute guy. I'd seen him earlier that night dancing with all ... I mean, he was constantly surrounded by women.

And I hadn't gotten a chance to talk to him, but I'd noticed him.

(Pause.)

So we were all lying in the dark, so I couldn't quite tell if ... but then my eyes started adjusting and I said: holy ... this guy lying next to me is ... this adorable guy is just staring at me and smiling at me.

And we just lay there smiling at each other for the next couple of hours.

Not touching or ...

I don't even remember when we fell asleep.

And the next morning we woke up, smiled at each other again, and he said: I'm James.

SCHULTZ. *(Softly.)*

I knew it.

MARTY. And I said: I'm Marty.

And he said ... I couldn't believe the ... without any kind of ... he just said, with total ... "Wanna go camping with me tomorrow? I'm driving north to Arcata."

I couldn't believe the nerve of this guy! And I had all these obligations back in ...

But I found myself saying ... I just said:

"Sure. Why not."

(James grins, embarrassed. Schultz applauds a little. A long pause.)

THERESA. That is really really cute.

(Another pause.)

MARTY. Okay. Who else has a story? And don't forget to really listen, you guys. We're gonna have to remember these.

(A terrified silence.)

THERESA. I'll go.
MARTY. Perfect.

(Theresa stands up, somewhat unnecessarily.)

THERESA. Okay. Well. This one time when I was still living in New York? I was on the … there was this old Jewish guy in my subway car. I knew he was Jewish because … well, he was stereotypically Jewish. I mean, not that all Jews look this way, obviously, but he had this humongous nose and this long like white beard with these big glasses and he had this accent like an old Jewish Yiddish-y Brooklyn accent and these … um … suspenders kind of pants.
    Anyway.
    The point is he was very clearly Jewish and he was sitting there talking to these old black guys. Who seemed kind of crazy. They all seemed crazy. But he was holding these pamphlets and he was yelling at them, not angry, just kind of yelling all this stuff and they were nodding and saying like, "Totally, man" or like, "You're so right" and I started listening and he was talking about this Jewish conspiracy and he used the phrase "Jew S.A." And then he was like: "Do you think the World Trade Towers came down by themselves?" And then he was talking about how, you know, the Jews killed Christ, and then … ah … what else. Oh. Something about World War II. How that happened because Jews were running Wall Street and Wall Street paid for Germany or something?

(A very long, weird silence. No one knows what to do.)

THERESA. I guess that's it.

(She sits down.)

MARTY. What made you think of that story?
THERESA. Um. I don't know. I think about it when … you know. The issue of self-hate or whatever.

(Pause.)

MARTY. That man may not have been Jewish.
THERESA. Oh. Um. I'm pretty sure he was.
MARTY. He may have fit your stereo … he may have fit your stereotype of a Jewish person, but he may not have been Jewish.

(Another silence. Finally Marty looks at her watch.)

MARTY. Okay. It looks like we're out of time!

(Everyone starts getting up.)

MARTY. Thanks, you guys.
    I think this was a really, really great start.

(They all start going over to the corner to get their bags, put on their shoes, turn on their cell phones, etc.)

MARTY. Hey — Lauren? I almost forgot. Just before you — I think you still owe me a check?
LAUREN. My mom was supposed to mail it to you.
MARTY. I don't think I … would you be willing to remind her?
LAUREN. Um. Yeah. Sure.

(Blackout.)

WEEK TWO

I

Lauren is standing center stage, facing the audience. Everyone else sits downstage, facing Lauren.

LAUREN. Hi.

My name is Schultz.

I'm a carpenter.

And I don't just ... I mean, I do regular carpenter things but I also make these amazing chairs that are like ... this one chair has, like ... like the headrest is the sun and the whole thing is gold?

(Lauren looks nervously at Schultz.)

It's kind of hard to explain.

There's this other chair that looks like a cloud.

Um ... I'm forty-eight years old.

I grew up in Maryland and my mom died when I was really little. She was an elementary school teacher. I always wanted to be a baseball player.

Um ...

I'm really nice to everyone.

(Pause.)

I met my wife Becky right out of college and we ...

(Schultz is saying something we can't hear.)

Yeah. I know. I was gonna —

We just separated. Divorced.

I'm in a lot of pain about it.

But, um, to look on the bright side, I have more time now to work on my chairs and maybe find a way for them to um, spread out to um, more people.

(Pause.)

I am an artist.

I am a really good artist.

(Blackout.)

II

Schultz, James, Theresa, and Lauren are playing a particularly confusing and chaotic version of Explosion Tag while Marty sits on her yoga ball. Explosion Tag is basically regular tag, except you're supposed to "explode" when tagged. When you're tagged you also become It, and as It you're supposed to be exploding constantly. When the lights come up Lauren is It. Everyone is awkwardly darting around the room. Lauren is exploding vocally, not physically (she keeps saying "powccchrrrpowpow"), and half-heartedly scurrying after people. Everyone has a different way of eluding her, although it is not very difficult. This can last up to a minute. Finally Lauren tags Theresa on the elbow. It is unclear whether or not Theresa purposely let this happen.

LAUREN. You're It.

(Theresa explodes balletically for a while, then tags Schultz, who is thrilled to be touched by her. Schultz makes a melodic falling bomb sound ["NEEEEEEeeeeerrrr"] while sinking to his knees. There is a long pause while he remains there, still. Everyone stops and watches. Finally Schultz explodes: silently, beautifully, atomically. His arms are thrust out, his eyes are wide open, his mouth is gaping open in a silent scream.)

MARTY. … Gorgeous.

(Schultz falls backwards onto the floor and lies on his back. There is a long silence while everyone remains standing, watching him.)

MARTY. You're It now, Schultz.
SCHULTZ. *(Sitting up.)*
Oh. Sorry.

(Schultz reaches out, quick as a snake, and grabs James' ankle.)

JAMES. Ah! Jesus.
SCHULTZ. You're It.

(Blackout.)

III

Breaktime.

Marty and Theresa are squatting by their bags in the corner, talking quietly. Schultz is lurking in the other corner, drinking from his water bottle.

THERESA. It's natural.
MARTY. It *is?*
THERESA. Weird, right?
MARTY. Well. It's beautiful.
THERESA. Thanks.
MARTY. Have you …
    (A pause.)
    I just … I saw them in CVS the other day, and I … have you seen these things?
THERESA. Wait, what are you talking about?
MARTY. These um … they're like these little packets of dye, but they're …
    (She giggles, then whispers.)
    They're for … it's for *pubic* hair.
THERESA. Oh my god.
MARTY. They were in their own little section, and I was: I said: Oh. My. God. and I called James over and he said: what's the big deal?
THERESA. Well. Of / course. He —
MARTY. And I was in a huff about it, I was in this big huff, and then I thought …

(Marty stops talking and glances over at Schultz.)

THERESA. *(Giggling.)*
Can you hear us, Schultz?

(Schultz lowers his water bottle.)

SCHULTZ. What? No.

(Marty and Theresa dissolve into more giggles. Schultz looks tormented.)

SCHULTZ. I have to check my uh ... my phone messages.

(Schultz takes his cell phone out of his pocket, crosses to the front corner of the room, and pretends [convincingly] to listen to a message.)

THERESA. So you were really angry —
MARTY. I was in a big huff about it, but then I ... oh god. You probably don't have to worry about this. You're too young. But my um ... that hair is half-*gray* now and it drives me crazy ... and I /
thought —
THERESA. Did you buy it?
MARTY. I'm thinking about it.
THERESA. Oh my god. Awesome.
MARTY. But then James will ... I know he's going to accuse me of being a hypocrite.
THERESA. I bet he'll like it.
MARTY. Theresa.
THERESA. I bet he will.

(Marty shakes her head.)

MARTY. I have to pee.

(Marty gets up and exits. Silence. Schultz is still listening to the imaginary message. Theresa smiles at him.)

THERESA. Hey.

(Schultz snaps his phone shut.)

SCHULTZ. Hi.

THERESA. How was your week?
SCHULTZ. It was okay.

(Pause.)

SCHULTZ. How was your week?
THERESA. It was good.
   (Pause.)
   I bought a plant!
SCHULTZ. Oh yeah? What kind?
THERESA. Um … I don't know. The tag says that it's a "money plant"? Like if you put it under — if you put it in the window you'll make a lot of money or something.
SCHULTZ. Wow.

(Silence.)

THERESA. Who called you?
SCHULTZ. My friend.
THERESA. Oh.

(Another silence. Theresa looks at the door, then back at Schultz.)

THERESA. So what do you think?
SCHULTZ. I ah…?
THERESA. About the class.
SCHULTZ. Huh. Well …
   (He glances nervously towards the door.)
   Uh … I like it. I don't feel … I guess I'm having a little trouble feeling totally comfortable?
THERESA. Yeah.
SCHULTZ. I feel pretty self-conscious.
THERESA. You'll get the hang of it.
SCHULTZ. You seem so … you're so good at everything.
THERESA. Well. I'm / actually —
SCHULTZ. You do everything in such a … you're so graceful.
THERESA. Oh god. That's …

(She shakes her head and grins. They look at each other. A long silence.)

THERESA. Schultz.
SCHULTZ. What.
THERESA. Do you maybe wanna get a cup of coffee after class?
Or um …

(Schultz stands there, speechless. Theresa is confused. After a long pause:)

THERESA. I'm sorry. Did I do something wrong?
SCHULTZ. No.
    I mean yes.
    Didn't I say yes?
THERESA. You didn't say anything.
SCHULTZ. Oh god. Yes.
    I'm sorry. I thought I said yes.
    Yes!

(Blackout.)

IV

James, Schultz, Theresa, and Lauren are sitting up against the stage right wall. Marty is in the center of the room, facing them.

MARTY. Okay. So I'm going to use myself as an example.

(They all nod. Marty taps her chin thoughtfully.)

MARTY. Schultz.
SCHULTZ. Yes.
MARTY. Will you be my father?
SCHULTZ. Gladly.

(He stands up. She takes hold of his arm and leads him into the center of the room.)

MARTY. *(To the group.)*

Don't be afraid to physically take hold of people and guide them. That's the point. Okay.

(Pause, to Schultz.)

All right. Um ... let's see. You are ... you're ... you're a very condescending ...

You're always kind of quietly Looking Down on everyone. So maybe ...

(Marty manipulates Schultz's arms until they're folded across his chest. Schultz is thoroughly enjoying himself.)

And also ... you have this certain ...

(She reaches up and pushes his eyebrows.)

You have a condescending sort of ...

(Schultz raises his eyebrows in exaggerated contempt.)

Perfect.

Okay. Stay that way.

(She turns back to the group.)

Now. Theresa. I want you to be my mother.

THERESA. Awesome.

(Theresa leaps up. Marty guides her towards the center of the room and puts her next to Schultz.)

MARTY. Okay. You are ... you're very angry. You're this very aggressive, very dominating woman ... people have always asked so much of you and not respected your intelligence and so you're really ...

(Marty manipulates Theresa's hands so that she's clutching her own hair.)

And if you could turn toward Schultz ... your husband ...

(Theresa turns towards Schultz.)

And ...

(Marty takes hold of Theresa's mouth. This surprises Theresa a little.)

And just ... you're screaming at him.

Good. Good.

And Lauren?

LAUREN. *(Not getting up.)*

Yeah.

MARTY. You're me.

(A pause.)

MARTY. Can you get up?

(Lauren gets up. This time Marty doesn't go over and take her arm. Instead Lauren slowly walks towards the center of the room.)

MARTY. I want you to sit on the ground.

(Lauren sits cross-legged on the ground.)

MARTY. Except I want you to hug your knees.

(Lauren obeys.)

MARTY. Yep. And kind of bury your head in …
    Yep.

(Marty observes for a while.)

MARTY. That looks great.

(She looks over at James, who is still seated against the wall.)

MARTY. Don't they look great?

(He nods. Silence.)

MARTY. Wow.
    Okay. You can relax.

(Theresa and Schultz exhale and let their arms drop to their sides, laughing. Lauren lifts her head up a little but doesn't move otherwise.)

SCHULTZ. Can I go next?
MARTY. Of course! Yes. Everyone back at the wall.

(Everyone starts heading back to the wall.)

MARTY. And this is just the beginning! Next week we start reenactments.

(Blackout.)

V

They are all lying on the floor again. The lights are dimmed.

SCHULTZ. One.
MARTY. Two.
THERESA. Three.

(Long silence.)

THERESA. Four.

(Silence.)

SCHULTZ. FIVE.

(Silence.)

JAMES. Six.

(Silence.)

SCHULTZ and LAUREN. Seven.
MARTY. Start again.

(Silence. Blackout.)

WEEK THREE

I

Schultz, center stage, facing the audience. Everyone else sits downstage, facing Schultz.

SCHULTZ. My name is Theresa.
Ah … I am a very special person.
(He looks tenderly in Theresa's direction.)
I am 35 years old.
I'm very passionate. About all things. I care about things very deeply.
(Pause.)
I grew up in a small town in New Hampshire. I have a younger brother named Brendan. He's getting married next summer.
Ah … I lived in New York for about … for many years. I was … I am an actress. The decision to move to Vermont was a difficult but I think ultimately positive one. There was a competitiveness and a claustrophobia that was very difficult for me in New York … also this sense that people didn't really care about each other.
(He shoots another tender look at Theresa.)
I have always wanted to make a difference. I have an amazing soul, an amazing warmth, that, that, that people can sense the minute they meet me. I had hoped to reach people through theater, but the realization that maybe this was impossible caused me to reevaluate and try living in a, a smaller place, where I could work, uh, directly with people. I'm studying for a certificate in acupressure and, ah …
Shoot.
Rolfing.
Rolfing.
About six months before I left New York I broke up with my

boyfriend, Mark. He was not very good to me. Sometimes I guilt myself out and convince myself that I ruined something and that I made a mistake, but those, uh, my friends and people who are close to me know that I did the right thing. That was a toxic relationship.

My father has prostate cancer. It's a, ah, blessing to be only a few hours away from him and to be able to see him on the weekends. I'm also worried about my mother.

I don't want my parents to die.

(A long pause while he thinks deeply about this.)
Yeah. Okay. That's it.

(Blackout.)

II

Theresa, James, and Lauren are standing against the wall. Schultz is standing in the center of the room, whispering to Marty. She nods, smiling.

MARTY. … Okay.
Yeah.
Yes. Beautiful.

(He thinks, then whispers something again.)

MARTY. Sure.

(She turns and smiles at Theresa, James and Lauren.)

MARTY. We're just figuring this out.

(Schultz whispers something to her again.)

MARTY. Well. Either way.

(Schultz nods. Marty walks back to the wall and stands against it with Lauren, Theresa, and James. A long silence while Schultz stands there, looking around the room, troubled.)

MARTY. Why don't you start with your bed.
SCHULTZ. *(To James.)*
　　Will you be my bed?
JAMES. Ah …
　　(He looks at Marty.)
　　Sure.

(James steps forward.)

MARTY. What did your bed look like?
SCHULTZ. … It was small.
　　(Pause.)
　　It was next to my window.
MARTY. Can you describe some of the … some of its special qualities to James?

(A silence.)

SCHULTZ. Small.
　　(Pause.)
　　Soft.

(Marty looks at James. Slowly, a little creakily, James gets on his hands and knees. They all watch him.)

MARTY. Great. What's next?
SCHULTZ. Ah —
MARTY. What's something you loved about your childhood bedroom?
SCHULTZ. … The tree outside my window.
MARTY. Perfect.
SCHULTZ. *(To Theresa.)*
　　Will you be the tree?
THERESA. Of course.

(Theresa steps forward.)

THERESA. What kind of tree?
SCHULTZ. Ah … maple.
THERESA. Am I large or small?
SCHULTZ. Large.

(Theresa stands near James and strikes a beautiful tree pose.)

SCHULTZ. Oh. Yeah.

(Schultz and Theresa smile at each other. To Lauren:)

SCHULTZ. Ah … will you be my baseball glove?
LAUREN. Um …
MARTY. What are some of the qualities of your baseball glove
that you'd like Lauren to embody?
SCHULTZ. Uh …

*(Lauren walks over to Theresa and James and plops down on the
ground, cross-legged.)*

SCHULTZ. Yeah. Okay.
MARTY. What else, Schultz? What else did you love about your
bedroom?
SCHULTZ. Ah …
　　(Pause.)
　　My stuffed snake.
MARTY. Your —
SCHULTZ. Right before she died my mother, uh … she gave me
this stuffed animal. A, ah … a stuffed snake.

(Pause.)

MARTY. Do you want me / to —
SCHULTZ. Yeah.
MARTY. Where do you want me to go?
SCHULTZ. Will you sit on my bed?

*(Marty nods. She sits on James' back, and mimes, as best she can, the
position of a stuffed snake.)*

MARTY. *(Still in stuffed snake position.)*
Okay. Now ... take a step back ... and look at your bedroom.

(Schultz takes a step back. They all freeze in their positions. He looks at them for a while.)

MARTY. What are you feeling?
SCHULTZ. Ah ...
(Pause.)
It doesn't really ...
I'm sorry.
(Pause.)
I ah ...
It doesn't really look like my bedroom.
MARTY. Does it feel like your bedroom?

(Schultz shakes his head. A sad silence.)

MARTY. ... Well. Okay.
SCHULTZ. Sorry.
MARTY. No. No. It's fine.

(She gets off of James' back, a little embarrassed.)

MARTY. Let's um ... we can all ... everybody can relax.

(James and Lauren get up immediately. Schultz smiles at Theresa.)

SCHULTZ. You were great.

(Blackout.)

III

Breaktime.

Theresa is by herself, sitting by her bag, listening to her messages. Schultz enters. He walks over to her, touches her hair, then kneels down and tries to kiss her.

THERESA. Hold on. I have to finish listening to my —

(Schultz keeps trying to kiss her.)

THERESA. Schultz. Hold on a second.

(Schultz stops and waits. After a second she snaps her phone shut. They look at each other. After a second, he leans in again and they kiss. She stops and looks nervously around the room.)

SCHULTZ. They're out feeding the meter.
THERESA. What about Lauren?
SCHULTZ. *(Softly.)*
    I thought about you this morning.
    In the shower.

(They begin to kiss again. After a few seconds Lauren walks in, sees them, freezes, and walks out. They don't see her. After more kissing:)

THERESA. … Oh god.
    Okay.
    We have to stop.

(Schultz looks at his watch.)

SCHULTZ. We have three more minutes.
THERESA. Schultz.
SCHULTZ. Come into the bathroom with me.

THERESA. I think that's probably a bad / id —
SCHULTZ. Just for a minute.
　　Just for a minute.

(He starts walking out the door. A little reluctantly, Theresa follows. The room is empty for twenty-five seconds. Then Lauren reenters, looking a little traumatized. She puts her bag down. She isn't sure what to do. She stands facing the mirrors, looking at herself. She frowns, then walks closer and inspects a pimple on her chin. After a little while Marty enters, looking at her phone. She sees Lauren and smiles.)

MARTY. Hey Lauren.
LAUREN. … Hey.
MARTY. Are you excited about school starting in a few weeks?
LAUREN. Um.
　　I'm not sure.

(Marty laughs a little.)

MARTY. That's understandable. I guess school is a mixed bag.

(A long pause while Marty smiles at Lauren. Then Marty walks over to her bag in the corner and starts rummaging through it.)

LAUREN. *(Suddenly.)*
　　Hey.
　　Um.
　　I have a question.
MARTY. *(Looking up.)*
　　Yes.
LAUREN. Um …

(A long silence.)

LAUREN. Are we going to be doing any real acting?

(Another silence.)

MARTY. … What do you mean by "real acting"?

LAUREN. Um …

> *(Pause.)* Like acting out a play. Or something. I don't know.
> *(Pause.)*
> Like reading from a …
> *(Pause.)*

MARTY. Um. Well. Honestly? I don't think so.

(Another silence.)

LAUREN. Okay.
MARTY. Did you … were you looking forward to that?
LAUREN. Um … I signed up for this class because I thought we were gonna act.
MARTY. We are acting.
LAUREN. … Yeah.

> *(Pause. She sighs.)*
> Okay. Thanks.

(Lauren exits. Marty watches her go. After a few seconds James enters.)

JAMES. She won't pick up. Her phone is on. She just won't pick up.
MARTY. Do you want me to call her?
JAMES. No. That's absurd.

> *(Pause.)*
> She's so fucking *ungrateful.*

MARTY. I don't know if I agree with that assessment.
JAMES. Okay. Could you please —

(Schultz and Theresa enter holding hands. Theresa drops Schultz's hand the second she sees other people in the room, then goes over to her bag and starts looking through it. Schultz is smiling. James looks at Schultz.)

JAMES. What.
SCHULTZ. Sorry?
JAMES. You're smiling like something … like something hilarious just happened.
SCHULTZ. Oh. Ah … no. Sorry.

(Blackout.)

IV

James and Theresa, standing, facing each other. Schultz and Lauren and Marty watch.

JAMES. *(Hello.)*
  Ak Mak.
THERESA. *(Hello.)*
  Goulash.
JAMES. Ak Mak?
THERESA. Ah … goulash. Goulash.
JAMES. Ak. Mak.

(James giggles.)

MARTY. Stay in it.
THERESA. *(Becoming serious — "I have something to tell you")*
  Goulash … goulash goulash goulash.
JAMES. *(What is it.)*
  Ak Mak.
THERESA. *(Sometimes, at night, I feel incredibly lonely.)*
  Goulash, goulash, goulash goulash goulash.
JAMES. *(I don't understand what you're saying)*
  Ak mak, Ak mak.
THERESA. *(I lie in bed staring at the ceiling, and I think about couples and families, like you and Marty.)*
  Goulash goulash goulash goulash, goulash goulash goulash goulash, goulash goulash goulash goulash.
JAMES. *(You are very beautiful.)*
  Ak mak, ak mak ak mak ak mak.
THERESA. *(Are you sad, too?)*
  Goulash?
JAMES. *(I am attracted to you.)*
  Ak mak.
THERESA. *(You're sad, too. I knew it.)*
  Goulash goulash goulash. Goulash.

JAMES. (*I feel really guilty when I think about how attracted I am to you.*)
  Ak mak ak mak ak mak ak mak.

(*A long silence.*)

THERESA. (*I feel like you understand me.*)
  Goulash goulash.
JAMES. (*I feel like you actually understand me.*)
  Ak mak ak mak.

(*They gaze at each other.*)

MARTY. Okay. Good. Stop. What were they communicating?
SCHULTZ. … They seemed very connected.
MARTY. Uh-huh. Good.
LAUREN. They were in love.

(*A weird pause.*)

LAUREN. It seemed like they were in love.

(*Another weird pause.*)

MARTY. Huh.
  Okay.
  Um … what was actually happening, though? What was being sad? Sorry. Said. What was being said?
SCHULTZ. Uh … well … I mean, the sentiment / was —
LAUREN. At first she seemed upset.
SCHULTZ. It seemed like she was sharing a secret.
LAUREN. Yeah. Like a …
SCHULTZ. But I thought that … it felt like James understood her.
THERESA. (*Softly.*)
  I'm sorry. Excuse me.

(*She quickly walks out of the room and shuts the door. Silence.*)

JAMES. Should / someone —

SCHULTZ. I will.
MARTY. No. That's okay.
    I'll be right back.

(She walks out of the room and shuts the door. Blackout.)

V

*The group stands in a circle. Theresa starts swinging her arms
back and forth and making a corresponding sound.*

THERESA. WOOP.
    WOOP.
    WOOP.
    WOOP.
MARTY. Let's all mirror it back to her!

*(Everyone mirrors the gesture/sound back to Theresa, in unison. After
a few seconds of this:)*

MARTY. Now Lauren! Transform it!

*(Lauren, after a second of hesitation, transforms the gesture/sound into
a different gesture/sound. The whole group mirrors it back to her. They
go around the circle, twice, playing Circle Mirror Transformation.
This is the only improvised part of the play. Except: the exercise should
end with Schultz transforming someone's else gesture into a form of solemn
and silent davening. Everyone silently davens on their knees for a while.)*

(Blackout.)

WEEK FOUR

I

Schultz enters the room, in darkness. He is the first one there. He switches on the lights. He puts his backpack down, drinks some water, gives himself a long look in the mirror, and then starts doing knee bends and touching his toes. Theresa enters, carrying her hula hoop. She starts a little when she sees Schultz.

THERESA. Hey.
SCHULTZ. Hey.

(A very long, agonized silence.)

THERESA. I'm sorry I didn't / call you last —
SCHULTZ. You don't need to apologize.

(Silence.)

THERESA. I know I don't.

(Silence.)

THERESA. But I'm sorry I didn't call you back.
SCHULTZ. Twice.
THERESA. What?
SCHULTZ. You didn't call me back twice.
THERESA. … I'm sorry.

(Schultz shrugs and takes a long drink from his water. Theresa watches him for a while.)

THERESA. You seem angry.

(Schultz lowers the water bottle and sighs.)

SCHULTZ. Um … I think I'm … I think I'm a little disappointed.
In you.
But. Uh. I'm not *angry*.

(A long silence.)

THERESA. Well. You shouldn't be disappointed in me.
(Pause.)
Because I've made it … I've made it really, really clear that
I / can't —
SCHULTZ. Yes. Thank you. Okay.
THERESA. Schultz.
SCHULTZ. It's just … it's funny. The not-calling.
Because a week and a half ago you were calling me every day.

(Pause.)

THERESA. Yeah.
SCHULTZ. So … it's just …
(Pause.)
I'm at a really vulnerable place in my life right / now, and —
THERESA. So am I!
SCHULTZ. — And the, uh, I really don't need someone who —
someone who's going to be inconsistent?

(Silence.)

THERESA. I'm sorry.

(Schultz convulses in horrible, strained, silent laughter.)

THERESA. I won't be … I won't be inconsistent anymore.
I think we … I think the best thing might be for … maybe we
should take a break from seeing each other. Outside of … and then
I won't have to —

*(The door opens. It's Marty and James and Lauren. They all come in
together, with their purses, backpacks, etc. Lauren and Marty are in*

the middle of a tense exchange.)

LAUREN. She said she mailed it to you three weeks ago.
MARTY. Okay. Sure. But I never got it.
LAUREN. Maybe it got lost in the mail.
MARTY. All right. Fine. But then she has to cancel it and ...

(Marty notices Theresa and Schultz.)

MARTY. Is everything okay?

THERESA. *(After a pause.)*
Mm-hm.

(Blackout.)

II

Theresa, center stage, beaming, facing the audience. Everyone else sits downstage, facing Theresa.

THERESA. I'm James.
I grew up in a lot of different places because my father was in the army. Um ... Germany. Chicago. Florida. I spent the last, um, three years of high school in Long Beach, California, so that was nice 'cause I got to graduate with people I knew and make real friends.
I went to school at UC Santa Barbara, which was pretty crazy in the late sixties! I learned a lot about myself during college. One, it was pretty hard to break away from my father and all his expectations for me. I also learned a lot about women and men and sexual politics.
Um ... I have a really funny story about avoiding the draft ... *(She glances briefly at James and grins.)*
But, um, okay.
I traveled around a lot after college. I lived in Monterey. I lived

at this crazy campground and I had to um, when I did my laundry I would hang my clothes out on the tree branches. Um ... I went to law school. That was a really different world. But I got really interested on my own in, um, Marxist philosophy, and, um, oh ... I met my first wife there. Her name was Sylvia. We got married a couple of years later. Um ... what else. Oh, god.

There's just a lot of good stuff.

I'm really interesting.

(She giggles.)

Um. Okay. I got through law school and I landed myself this really, like, great job at a firm in Berkeley and then the day of the bar exam came and I went there and I sat down at the desk and I looked down at the paper in front of me and then I just, like, put down my pencil and I walked out.

Because I realized at that moment that I didn't want to participate in that. In the system. I didn't want to contribute to, like, a fundamentally flawed ...

(A pause, she glances at Marty.)

Oh god. Okay. Sorry. I'll stop um ...

I have a daughter! Her name is Erin. She's my only child but I wish we were a little closer ...

(Theresa sobers up a little.)

And that's hard for me.

She's close with Marty. Marty is my wife.

(She grins at Marty.)

Marty is *awesome*.

We live in this amazing house near the center of town painted these really amazing colors. It's like purple and orange and yellow and people stop their cars and take pictures of it. We have a cat named Coltrane.

Coltrane only has three legs.

(She giggles again.)

Um ... okay.

I am ...

(She sobers up and thinks again.)

I am a very strong man. By strong I don't mean physically strong, although, um, that too. I've been through a lot. My first wife was an alcoholic. My whole family is alcoholics. Alcoholic. My father was emotionally abusive to my mother and although I'm not that way I feel a lot of his anger inside of me. I feel it and

I think instead of dealing with it I push it, um, I push it deep down inside me and repress it.

(A pause.)

But the truth is ... I mean, I haven't said this. But ...

I think the problem is not my father so much as my fear of being my father. Like if I run away too hard from him I will become something else that is also problematic.

Because actually?

I'm an amazing person.

(She grins.)

Okay. Thank you.

(Blackout.)

III

Lights up. Theresa, Marty, Schultz, and James stand in a line. Lauren is facing them.

LAUREN. Um.

(Silence. Lauren steps forward. She taps James on the shoulder.)

LAUREN. You're my dad. Neil. You're Neil.
JAMES. Okay.
LAUREN. Just ... um ...

(She takes him by the arm and leads over to a different spot in the room.)

LAUREN. This is um. You're ... um. You're in an armchair. You're reading.

(James nods, sits on the yoga ball, and pretends to be studying an invisible newspaper. Lauren walks back over to Theresa and Marty and Schultz.)

LAUREN. Um.

(Lauren taps Marty on the shoulder.)

LAUREN. Will you be my mom?

(Marty nods, smiling. Lauren leads her to a spot in the room across from James.)

LAUREN. *(To Marty.)*
    You're um …
    You're angry.
MARTY. Why am I angry?
LAUREN. Um … because he's angry?

(A confused pause.)

JAMES. Should I just …
LAUREN. You should / just —
JAMES. Wait — what you said before? About / the —
LAUREN. Yeah.
MARTY. Why don't we start? And Lauren … you can stop us at any time.

(Lauren nods, then steps back. Silence.)

MARTY. Neil.

(James continues reading his invisible newspaper.)

MARTY. Neil. I need to talk to you about something.

(A pause while James studies his invisible newspaper. Then he looks up.)

JAMES. *(To Marty and Lauren.)*
    I'm sorry. I'm having a little — I'm kind of drawing a blank.
MARTY. Can you just go off what Lauren told you?
JAMES. I don't really … I don't really know who this guy is.
MARTY. … Can you try?
JAMES. Can I try to *what?*

(Marty sighs. A pause.)

JAMES. Never mind.
　　Start again.

(He goes back to reading his newspaper.)

MARTY. James. I mean, Neil.
　　Neil.
　　I need to talk to you.
JAMES. I'm busy.
MARTY. You're reading the newspaper.
JAMES. The newspaper is important to me.
MARTY. Please pay attention to me, Neil.

(After a second, James puts down his newspaper.)

JAMES. What is it?
MARTY. I'm lonely.
JAMES. Well, fine. I'm lonely, too. We're all lonely.
MARTY. Then why do you ignore us? Why do you insist on …
why are you always reading at the dinner table? Or watching TV
when you should be talking to Lauren?

(A pause.)

MARTY. Why don't you engage with me anymore?
JAMES. You're too neurotic.
LAUREN. *(From the corner.)*
　　He wouldn't say that. I mean, he wouldn't think that.
MARTY. What would he think / was —
LAUREN. He would say that she's always nagging him.
JAMES. *(To Marty.)*
　　You're always nagging me.
MARTY. Maybe I'm nagging you because you're ignoring me!
JAMES. Maybe I'm ignoring you because you're driving me crazy!

(A pause.)

MARTY. Then leave, Neil.

Why don't you just leave?

(Another pause.)

JAMES. I'm stuck.
MARTY. Well, I'm stuck, too.
JAMES. And I, uh …

(He is in pain. A long pause.)

MARTY. But what about Lauren? Just because you're mad at me doesn't mean you should … you can still be nice to your daughter!

(Another pause.)

JAMES. *(Softly.)*
    I'm worried she's going to judge me.
MARTY. She's not going to judge you. She loves you.
JAMES. I'm worried she's going to …

(James starts rubbing the spot between his eyes. It's unclear whether or not he's crying.)

JAMES. I, uh …
MARTY. What? Be straightforward for once!
JAMES. … I feel ashamed.
MARTY. Of what?
JAMES. Of what I've …
    (A long pause.)
    Of my life.
MARTY. But Lauren isn't judging you, Neil.
    (Pause.)
    She just wants you to love her.
    Neil. Look at me.

(James looks up, tears in his eyes.)

MARTY. Lauren just wants you to love her and pay attention to her.
    (Pause.)
    That's all you need to do.

(After a while, James nods. He and Marty look at each other sadly. After a while Marty breaks and looks at Lauren.)

MARTY. Well?

(Lauren purses her lips, thinking. Everyone waits nervously for her response. After a long silence:)

LAUREN. That was pretty good.

(Blackout.)

IV

Breaktime.

Theresa is alone, drinking from her Nalgene. The door opens. It's Schultz. He sees her, sees that she's the only one in the room, and then darts away, shutting the door behind him. Theresa sighs. The door opens again. It's James.

THERESA. Hi.
JAMES. Hi.

(James steps into the room and shuts the door behind him.)

JAMES. … That was intense.
THERESA. Yeah.

(A pause.)

THERESA. You got / pretty —
JAMES. I got kind of worked up.
THERESA. I mean, I think that's great. Maybe that's what Lauren needed.
JAMES. Yeah.

THERESA. She's a really sweet kid.

JAMES. Yeah.

She reminds me of my daughter. In some … in certain ways.

THERESA. Erin?

JAMES. Yeah. Good memory.

THERESA. Oh god. I never forget stuff like that. I mean, about people that I … people that I find interesting.

(Pause.)

My ex-boyfriend … I like totally memorized his entire life. I'd bring up some girl he kissed in high school and he'd be like: "Who?" and I'd be like: "Lopie Grossman, you made out with her twenty years ago" and he'd be like —

Jesus. That's actually her name.

See? I still remember.

JAMES. That's amazing.

THERESA. It's actually horrible.

(Pause.)

I'm like haunted by these …

(A pause.)

JAMES. So are you and Schultz…?

THERESA. Oh. No.

Yeah. No.

JAMES. Huh.

(Pause.)

THERESA. We were. For a little while. I mean, we went out on a / couple of —

JAMES. Yeah. I mean, I knew that.

(Pause.)

THERESA. That was a … I feel like such an asshole. It was a mistake and now … and now things are really weird. I shouldn't be talking to you about it.

(Theresa glances toward the door.)

JAMES. He said that you were still hung up on Mark?
THERESA. Schultz said that?
JAMES. Yeah.
THERESA. So / he —
JAMES. He called me and Marty the other night. He was really upset. He hadn't heard back from you and / he —
THERESA. Oh god. That's …
     Oh god. Poor Schultz. I'm such a …

(She shakes her head.)

JAMES. What?
THERESA. It's just … I mean, I *am* really screwed up about Mark. But it's like … I mean … I would … I would like to be, to try being in a relationship right now, you know?
     (Pause.)
     Just not with Schultz.
     Oh god. I hate myself.
JAMES. You shouldn't hate yourself.
     (Pause.)
     Was it … did you feel like he was too old for you?
THERESA. Oh. God. No. I always date older guys.

(An awkward silence. Theresa goes back to drinking from her Nalgene. James watches her.)

JAMES. You shouldn't hate yourself.

(Theresa smiles at him.)

THERESA. Aw. James. Well … thanks.
     You're really cool.

(James looks down.)

THERESA. You and Marty are like the coolest couple ever. I loved hearing all your … your stories and … it made me really happy. I was just like: this couple is so cool!
JAMES. Yeah. She —

(Lauren enters.)

LAUREN. Hi.
THERESA. Hey, Lauren.

(James nods. Lauren goes over to the corner, sits down, riffles through her backpack, and pulls out a wrapped sandwich. She slowly opens the sandwich and begins eating it, while curiously looking over at James and Theresa. They are self-conscious. After a while:)

THERESA. So tell me about Erin!
JAMES. Oh. Ah …

(James rubs his forehead.)

THERESA. How old is she?
JAMES. She's twenty-three.
THERESA. Okay. Cool.
JAMES. She actually ah … she refuses … she's refusing to, ah, *speak* to me right now.

(Lauren, still in the corner, stops chewing. James clears his throat.)

THERESA. Oh no. Um … can I ask / why —
JAMES. Marty, ah …
    (He shakes his head.)
    I guess it's not really Marty's fault.
THERESA. Uh-huh.
JAMES. Ah …
    (He lowers his voice.)
    About two months ago, she — Marty — told her something I wish she hadn't … Marty didn't — I don't know *why* she — but Marty didn't realize that Erin … That I hadn't told Erin about, ah … this ah … this, ah …
    (His voice drops even lower and quieter.)
    … very minor infidelity that I, ah, committed during my marriage to, ah, Erin's mother —
THERESA. Oh. Okay.
JAMES. — And ah … anyway Marty sort of brought it up on the phone in this sort of casual — I don't know *why* she — but that's

beside the — and Erin said: "Who's Luisa?"
THERESA. Oh. God.
JAMES. And now she's not speaking to me.
THERESA. Oh James.
JAMES. She is speaking to Marty.
THERESA. Well. That makes sense.
JAMES. Yeah. Ah ... does it?
THERESA. I'm sorry.
JAMES. Yeah. I just ah ...
THERESA. It'll get better.

(James nods. Lauren chews her sandwich and stares at them from her spot in the corner. Blackout.)

V

They are all lying on the floor again. The lights are dimmed.

THERESA. One.
JAMES. Two.

(Silence.)

MARTY. Three.
SCHULTZ. Four.

(Silence.)

SCHULTZ. Five.

(Silence.)

LAUREN. Six.
MARTY. Seven.

(Silence.)

JAMES. Eight.
THERESA and SCHULTZ. Nine.

(A very long, disappointed silence.)

JAMES. One.

(Silence.)

LAUREN. Two.

(Silence.)

SCHULTZ. Three.

(Silence.)

MARTY. Four.
LAUREN. *(Still lying on her back.)*
    I don't get it. I don't get what the point is.
MARTY. Lauren, maybe you should wait until after class to talk
to me about this.

(Lauren sits up abruptly.)

LAUREN. *(To Theresa.)*
    You were like a real actress. Why aren't you the teacher?

(Still lying down, Theresa shuts her eyes and shakes her head.)

LAUREN. What's the point of counting to ten?!
MARTY. The point is being able to be totally present. To not
get in your head and second-guess yourself. Or the people
around you.
LAUREN. I want to know how to become a good *actress*.
MARTY. That is how you become a good actress.
THERESA. She's right, Lauren.

*(Lauren looks at Theresa, wounded. After a few seconds she lies back
down. A long silence.)*

THERESA. One.
JAMES. Two.

(Silence.)

LAUREN. Three.
MARTY and SCHULTZ. Four.

(Blackout.)

WEEK FIVE

I

Marty, center stage, facing the audience. She has a small Band-Aid on her forehead. Everyone else sits downstage, facing Marty.

MARTY. My name is Lauren Zadick-White.

I'm sixteen.

I was born right before midnight, on October 24th. Um … I'm a Scorpio, and my mother says that accounts for why I'm such a hard worker.

Also why I'm so stubborn!

Ah … this fall I'll be a junior at Shirley High. School is okay, but I can't wait to go to college and start doing what I love, which is theater and dance. I'm also really interested in going to veterinary school. We'll see. I don't have to make any decisions right now, even though I think I do.

(She gazes pointedly at Lauren.)

I don't enjoy talking that much about my family and my, um, background, but it's actually fascinating and just … really, really interesting.

My mother is Lebanese, and my father is Irish. Both of them were born outside of the States and they met at the University of Iowa.

Um … my grandmother lives with us. We call her *Sitti.* That's Lebanese for "grandma." I'm really close with her. Everyone says we look alike.

(Pause.)

I have agreed to let all of you know that in the past couple of years my father has had some problems with the, um, law. I hope that this will remain strictly confidential. It has been really hard for my whole family, especially my mother and grandmother, who have always had such high expectations. My grandmother thinks my mother should leave my father. They fight about it.

(Pause.)

I'm not going to go into any more detail.

(Pause.)

It is really hard for me to talk about it and I should be so proud of myself for sharing it with all of you.

(Pause.)

Oh. Also. This fall they're doing *West Side Story* at the high school and I would really like to get the part of Maria. It's my dream role. I signed up for this class so I would be, um, better prepared for it.

(Pause.)

I hope that I …

Maybe one day I can stop putting so much pressure on myself.

(Blackout.)

II

James and Lauren and Marty are watching Theresa and Schultz, who stand in the center of the room facing each other.

THERESA. I want it.
SCHULTZ. You can't have it.

(Silence.)

THERESA. I want it.
SCHULTZ. You can't have it.
THERESA. I WANT IT.
SCHULTZ. You can't have it.
THERESA. I WANT IT.
SCHULTZ. You can't have it.
MARTY. Come on, Schultz. Really get into it.
THERESA. I want it.
SCHULTZ. Well, you can't have it.
THERESA. But I want it.

SCHULTZ. You can't have it.
THERESA. I FUCKING WANT IT!

(Silence.)

SCHULTZ. Jesus.

(Schultz wipes his mouth with his sleeve, a little upset. He puts his hands on his hips. Shaking his head.)

SCHULTZ. You can't have it.
MARTY. Switch phrases.
THERESA. I want to go.
SCHULTZ. … Wait, what do I say?
MARTY. "I need you to stay."
SCHULTZ. I need you to stay.
THERESA. Well, I want to go.

(Schultz regards Theresa sadly.)

SCHULTZ. I need you to stay.
THERESA. I want to go.
SCHULTZ. I need you to stay.
THERESA. But I / want to —
SCHULTZ. I need you to stay.
    (After a short pause.)
    I need you to stay.
MARTY. Good.
THERESA. I want to go.
SCHULTZ. I. Need. You. To. Stay.
THERESA. I want to go.

(Schultz runs forward and grabs Theresa by the shoulders.)

SCHULTZ. I NEED YOU TO STAY.
MARTY. Okay, no touching.
THERESA. I want to go.
    (To Marty.)
    I'm sorry. I need to go the bathroom.
    (To James.)

Will you step in for me?
JAMES. … Sure.

(Theresa exits quickly. Schultz and James stand facing each other. Blackout.)

III

Lauren and James are standing, facing each other. Theresa is hovering nearby, watching them. Schultz and Marty are leaning against the wall.

LAUREN. Stop haunting me, Mark.

(A pause.)

JAMES. You shouldn't have broken up with me.
    You made a mistake.
LAUREN. No I didn't.
JAMES. Yes you did.
LAUREN. No I didn't. You were domineering and you made me feel … you made me forget Who I Am.
JAMES. Who cares? Now you're going to be alone forever.
LAUREN. No I'm not.
JAMES. Yes you are.
LAUREN. No I'm not.
JAMES. Yes you are.
LAUREN. No I'm not.
JAMES. Yes you are.

(Silence.)

LAUREN. No I'm not.
MARTY. *(From the corner.)*
    Okay. Let's make it a little / more —
LAUREN. I'm not going to be alone forever.

JAMES. I'm the best guy you'll ever have, Theresa. I was the best guy you'll ever have.
LAUREN. You don't know that. Have you ... have you, like, met all the guys in the world?

(Pleased with herself, Lauren glances over at Theresa.)

JAMES. No one will ever love you the way that I do.
LAUREN. You were too possessive.
JAMES. That was one of the things you secretly liked about me.
LAUREN. *(Glancing over at Theresa.)*
     No it wasn't?

(Theresa shakes her head.)

LAUREN. Yes it was. Okay, yes it was, but that doesn't mean it was good for me. I am a beautiful, um, really cool woman and I'm really attractive and there are lots of men out there who will like me and be nice to me.
JAMES. You're fooling yourself.

(A pause. Lauren sighs.)

LAUREN. I don't know what I'm supposed to say.

(Theresa speaks up from the corner.)

THERESA. I don't want to be with a man who threatens me.
JAMES. I'm not threatening you. I'm telling you the truth.
THERESA. *(Stepping forward.)*
     No. That's not ... it's because you're insecure, Mark. You could never just let me love you and be free. You were so ... you were so judgmental and moralistic. You were always lecturing me. If you really love someone, you don't make them feel bad about themselves! All this negative stuff you're saying ... it's just ... it's just further proof that you don't really care about me the way that you say you do. If you really loved me, you'd want me to feel okay about the future. You'd want me to be optimistic.

(Silence. Then James smiles.)

JAMES. I'm speechless.

(Theresa grins.)

THERESA. Whew!
MARTY. That was great.
LAUREN. *(To Theresa.)*
   Sorry.
THERESA. No! You were awesome.
LAUREN. *(To Marty.)*
   He was starting to make me feel really bad.

(Theresa gives James a high five.)

THERESA. That was so crazy, man! You totally reminded me of him!

(James beams. Schultz watches all of this, expressionless. Blackout.)

IV

Breaktime.

Marty is alone in the room, standing in front of the mirrors, looking at her reflection and fussing a little with the Band-Aid on her forehead. After a while Schultz enters. He looks at her.

SCHULTZ. What happened?
MARTY. Oh. God. Yeah. It's … I fell out of bed. Two nights ago. If you can believe it.
SCHULTZ. Why?
MARTY. … Why what?
SCHULTZ. Why did you fall out of bed?
MARTY. Oh. Um … I don't know. I'm not sure what happened. I just woke up and I was on the floor. It's happened to me a bunch

of times in the past couple of years.
SCHULTZ. Are you a restless sleeper?
MARTY. Um —
SCHULTZ. Do you talk a lot? Wake up screaming?
MARTY. Well, James says I do. And the other week / I —
SCHULTZ. Night terrors.
MARTY. What?
SCHULTZ. You probably have night terrors.

(Marty smiles.)

SCHULTZ. It's a real thing, Marty.
MARTY. What is it?
SCHULTZ. Becky used to get them. They're uh … they're different from dreams because they're just … they're just fear. And they can make you have these like, these little seizures. And sometimes you fall out of bed.
MARTY. Huh.
SCHULTZ. Were you abused as a child?
MARTY. I'm sorry?
SCHULTZ. Were you abused as a child?
MARTY. … No. Um. No. I don't think so.
SCHULTZ. Okay. 'Cause it's a common symptom among abuse survivors.
MARTY. Huh.

(Pause.)

SCHULTZ. Night terrors.
MARTY. Huh. Yeah. Maybe. I don't know what it was.
SCHULTZ. It was night terrors.
MARTY. Yeah.
SCHULTZ. Becky went on medications for … she went on some kind of epilepsy medication. It helped her.
MARTY. Huh.

(Pause.)

MARTY. And it's a real —
SCHULTZ. It's a real thing. It's a real thing. Look it up online.

MARTY. Okay. Yeah. Thanks.

(*Silence.*)

MARTY. How're you doing, Schultz? Are you okay?

(*Pause.*)

SCHULTZ. Uh … I don't know.
  (*Pause.*)
  How are you?

(*James suddenly enters, exuberant, with a water bottle.*)

JAMES. I hooped.
  I hooped for over a minute.
MARTY. … Wow.
  Great.
JAMES. Now Theresa is giving Lauren a massage. In the parking lot. It's hilarious. You guys should go take a look.

(*Marty and Schultz both attempt to smile.*)

MARTY. … That's great.

(*James suddenly grabs Marty in his arms and gives her a kiss. It's a little awkward. Marty smiles at Schultz, embarrassed.*)

(*Blackout.*)

V

The entire group is sitting in a circle.

MARTY. When I go to India ... I'm going to bring my purple shawl.
LAUREN. Wait. I've played this before. Isn't it California? "When I go to California"? We played this in fifth grade.
MARTY. This time we're playing it with India.
　　When I go to India I will bring my purple shawl. Schultz?
SCHULTZ. I don't understand / what —
LAUREN. Say what she said and then add something.
　　(After a pause.)
　　"When I go to India I'm gonna bring my purple shawl and a," like, another object. Then the next person lists all the other things and adds on something new.
SCHULTZ. Ah ... when I go to India I'm gonna bring my purple shawl and ah ...

(A long silence.)

MARTY. Whatever you want.

(Another long silence.)

SCHULTZ. Phillips head screwdriver.
MARTY. Okay.
LAUREN. When I go to India I'm gonna bring a purple shawl and a Phillips head screwdriver and a ... a toothbrush.
MARTY. Theresa! Quick! And get creative!
THERESA. When I go to India I'm going to bring a purple shawl and a Phillips head screwdriver and a toothbrush and ... a tiny velvet cape.
LAUREN. *What?*
THERESA. Sorry. Just a cape. A velvet cape.
MARTY. Good! Keep going! James!
JAMES. When I go to India I'm gonna bring a ... a ... a purple

shawl and a Phillips head screwdriver and a toothbrush and a velvet cape and … ah …

The Bible.

MARTY. WhenIgotoIndiaI'mgonnabringapurpleshawlandaPhillips headscrewdriverandatoothbrushandavelvetcapeandacopyoftheBibl eand … a bottle of red wine!

(Pause.)

Schultz!

SCHULTZ. Okay.

I can do this.

(Pause.)

When I go to India I'm gonna bring a purple shawl and a Phillips head screwdriver and a toothbrush and a and a and a and a copy of the Bible and a … and a big ol' bottle of red wine! Yes! Oh. And a battle axe!

(A long pause.)

LAUREN. You forgot the velvet cape.
SCHULTZ. … I did?

(A pause.)

MARTY. Did he?
Who remembers?
LAUREN. He forgot.
JAMES. I didn't notice.
MARTY. Me neither.

(A silence, during which Theresa grapples with an ethical dilemma. Finally:)

THERESA. Um … I think he forgot.

(A wounded silence.)

MARTY. Okay. Um. Schultz, you're out.
SCHULTZ. What does that mean?
MARTY. You're just …
You have to leave the circle.

(After a while Schultz gets up. He stands there for a few seconds, then walks away from the circle. He wavers on his feet, clenching and unclenching his fists.)

MARTY. Whose turn is it?
LAUREN. Me.
    Um … When I go to India I'm gonna bring a purple ca — a purple shawl, a Phillips head screwdriver, a toothbrush …

(While Lauren is talking Schultz walks over to the wall of mirrors and stands there, making direct eye contact with his own reflection. He remains there, unmoving.)

LAUREN. … a velvet cape, a copy of the Bible … a bottle of red wine … and, um … a battle axe.
    And a calico kitten.
    (Pause.)
    I did it! Right? I did it!

(Marty, who has been glancing over in Schultz's direction, clears her throat.)

MARTY. You know what? I want us to try something different.
LAUREN. But —
SCHULTZ. *(Still facing his reflection, not moving.)*
    It's fine, Marty.
MARTY. No. No. I … I just forgot how competitive this game is. And it's … this … what we're doing in this class is really not about competition.

(Silence.)

MARTY. Schultz.
    Please come back and join us in the circle.

(Schultz slowly turns around and rejoins the circle.)

MARTY. Great. So this next exercise is … hm. Wait. We need paper.

(Marty gets up and hurries over to her backpack. She takes out a flyer and hurries back into the circle. She begins tearing the flyer into five strips.)

MARTY. Okay. We're going to … uhp. You know what? We also need pencils.

(She gets up again and hurries back over to her backpack, then rummages through it. They all watch her.)

MARTY. I've got one … two … three … this is usable, I guess … four …
JAMES. I've got a pen.
MARTY. Okay. Perfect.

(She returns to the circle.)

MARTY. So. Everyone take a …

(Marty hands out the pencils/pens.)

MARTY. Okay. So I want everyone to take your scrap of paper and write on it … I want you to write down a secret that you've never, ever told *anyone*.
LAUREN. Whoa.
MARTY. And … you don't have to be specific. We don't need to know it's you. In fact, we *shouldn't* know it's you. This is an opportunity to have people … to be able to air a secret in front of a group without feeling like you have to … like you have to answer to it. Or someone.

(Silence.)

THERESA. What if we don't have any secrets?
MARTY. You must have *one*.
THERESA. I don't know. I've been pretty open in all my relationships. I basically tell my partners everything.
MARTY. Okay. Well, if you can't — just try to think of something that … something that's hard for you to talk about.

(Theresa nods.)

MARTY. Okay. So. Just … don't take too long. Write down the first big thing that comes into your mind. Even if it's scary.

(They all nod.)

MARTY. All right. Go for it.

(Everyone [including Marty] starts writing/thinking/chewing on their pens/scootching away to a different part of the floor to have right amount of privacy to write/think/chew on their pens. Silence and then the sound of scribbling for about 45 seconds.)

MARTY. Is everyone done?
LAUREN. Just … hold on.
SCHULTZ. Yeah. I need a few more seconds.

(Mary waits for about 10 more seconds.)

MARTY. Okay. Now fold up your paper into four — fold it twice into a little square and give it back to me.

(They all obey.)

MARTY. And let's all sit together again.

(They return to the circle.)

MARTY. Okay.
    (She takes the little pieces of paper and shakes them in her cupped hands.)
    … We're each gonna pick one. And we're gonna stand in front of the group and read it silently to ourselves, and then we're gonna read it out loud to the group. In a very sincere … in a meaningful way.
SCHULTZ. What if you pick your own?
MARTY. Just read it anyway. We won't know.
    (Pause.)
    Okay?
    Trust me, guys.
    Lauren.

Pick one.

(Lauren picks a square of paper.)

MARTY. Okay … now …
    (She hands the papers out.)
    Schultz …
    James …
    Theresa …
    Okay.
    And I guess this one is for me.
    (Pause.)
    Um … Schultz. Can you stand up?

(Schultz stands up.)

MARTY. Will you deliver your secret, please?

(Schultz opens his piece of paper, reads it silently, and then looks up.)

SCHULTZ. My father may have molested me.

(A slightly shocked silence.)

MARTY. Okay. Thank you.

(Schultz sits down.)

MARTY. Theresa?

(Theresa stands up. She unfolds and looks at her piece of paper.)

THERESA. I secretly think I am smarter than everyone else in the world.

(A pause. Lauren giggles triumphantly.)

MARTY. Lauren.
    Great, Theresa. Good job.

(Theresa sits back down.)

MARTY. James?

(James slowly stands up, unfolds and then reads directly from his paper.)

JAMES. I have a problempossibleaddiction
    (He looks up.)
      ... that's written as one word...
      ... with Internet pornography.

(Lauren covers her mouth with her hand.)

MARTY. Great. Thank you.

(James sits back down.)

MARTY. Lauren?

(Lauren stands up. She reads her paper, then stuffs it into her pocket. She looks out at the group.)

LAUREN. I think I might be in love with Theresa.

(A very long silence. Lauren is still standing.)

LAUREN. Um ...
MARTY. You can sit down. Thank you.

(Lauren sits down. Another horrible 10-second silence. Schultz frowns, then looks traumatized, then stares angrily at James, then looks traumatized again.)

MARTY. Okay. Ah ...
    I guess it's my turn.

(Marty stands up. She unfolds her piece of paper and reads it out loud, not taking her eyes off the paper. Her voice is shaky.)

MARTY. Sometimes I think that everything I do is propelled by my fear of being alone.

(A very long silence. Marty finally crumples the paper in her fist. She refuses to make eye contact with anyone.)

MARTY. Great job, you guys.

(Blackout.)

VI

They are all lying on their backs in the semidarkness. Silence for a while.

MARTY. *(Dully.)*
  Okay. Next week is our last class. So let's really try to …

(A long silence.)

LAUREN. One.

(Silence.)

JAMES. Two.

(Silence.)

LAUREN. Three.

(Silence.)

THERESA. Four.
JAMES. Five.

(A long silence.)

SCHULTZ. Six.

(Silence.)

JAMES. Seven.
THERESA. Eight.
MARTY. Nine.

(A very, very long silence.)

LAUREN. Ten.

(No one moves. Blackout.)

WEEK SIX

I

*The room, in darkness. The sound of footsteps in the hall-
way. Marty enters the room, her bag over her shoulder, and
turns on the lights. She stands there for a while, tired. She
walks over to the corner of the room and puts her bag down.
She walks over to the yoga ball and sits down. She bounces
there, sadly, for about 15 seconds. The door opens. James
enters. Marty stops bouncing. James walks over to the corner and puts his bag down. He stands there in the corner,
looking at her. She stays on the ball. They look at each other
for a while.*

MARTY. You came.
JAMES. Of course.

(She nods. Silence for a while.)

JAMES. I talked to Erin the other night. Finally.

(Marty nods.)

JAMES. She said you didn't call her back this week. That she left
you / five —
MARTY. So that's good. So you talked to each other.

(He nods. More silence.)

JAMES. How's Phyllis?
MARTY. Fine.

(Silence.)

JAMES. So what are you …
     Are you on the *couch* / or —
MARTY. There's an air mattress.

(More silence.)

JAMES. Come home, Marty.
MARTY. No fucking way.

(Another silence.)

JAMES. You … did you want this to happen or something?
MARTY. Did I *what*?
JAMES. Having us write out —
     Did you *want* me / to —
MARTY. Okay. See. That's exactly. That's exactly the problem.
     That right there.

(The door opens. It's Schultz, with his backpack.)

SCHULTZ. Hi, guys.
JAMES. Hey, Schultz.

(Schultz steps inside and puts his backpack down in the corner.)

SCHULTZ. How were your — did you guys have a good week?

(Marty and James both nod. Awkward silence for a little while. Schultz unzips his backpack and takes out a little box.)

SCHULTZ. Ah … Marty?
MARTY. Mm-hm?
SCHULTZ. I wanted to, uh …

(Schultz walks over to Marty and hands her the little box.)

SCHULTZ. Thanks.
MARTY. Oh, Schultz.
SCHULTZ. For everything. It's been a great class.

(Marty looks down at the box.)

MARTY. Should I —
SCHULTZ. Yeah. Open it.

(Marty rips off the paper and takes the lid off the box.)

MARTY. Oh wow.

(She stares at the box's contents.)

SCHULTZ. Yep.
MARTY. This is really great.
SCHULTZ. Do you already have one?
MARTY. Um … well, yes, I do, but it's bigger, and not as nice. It's in the living room.
JAMES. *(From across the room.)*
    What is it?
SCHULTZ. It's a dreamcatcher.
MARTY. We can put this one …
    I can put this one in the …

(Marty trails off. She lifts the dreamcatcher out of the box and holds it up to the light.)

MARTY. I love the little purple —
SCHULTZ. Ah man. I was hoping you didn't already have one.
MARTY. No. No. I love it. I love it.

(Marty puts it back in the box.)

SCHULTZ. The Native Americans used them to uh …

(An awkward silence. He has forgotten.)

MARTY. Thank you so much, Schultz.
SCHULTZ. Maybe it'll help with the night terrors.
MARTY. Mm-hm.
SCHULTZ. Night terror catcher.

(Schultz looks at James.)

SCHULTZ. Did she tell you about those?

(James shakes his head. Blackout.)

II

They are all sitting in a circle.

MARTY. If
LAUREN. I
SCHULTZ. Wanted
THERESA. To
JAMES. Become
MARTY. A
LAUREN. ... Actress
SCHULTZ. I
THERESA. Would
JAMES. Just
MARTY. Go
LAUREN. *(Pause.)*
    Home.
SCHULTZ. ... I
THERESA. Have
JAMES. Learned
MARTY. So
LAUREN. Um ... Much.
SCHULTZ. *(Pause.)*
    I
THERESA. Will
JAMES. Try
MARTY. To
LAUREN. Realize
SCHULTZ. The
THERESA. Gigantic-ness!

JAMES. Of
MARTY. Capabilities!
LAUREN. And
SCHULTZ. The
THERESA. Way
JAMES. I
MARTY. Express
LAUREN. Anger
SCHULTZ. Is
THERESA. … Indescribable.
JAMES. Peace
MARTY. Is
LAUREN. Just
SCHULTZ. Okay
THERESA. For
JAMES. Everybody
MARTY. But
LAUREN. We
SCHULTZ. Will
THERESA. Succeed
JAMES. Always
MARTY. If
LAUREN. We
SCHULTZ. Try
THERESA. And
JAMES. Become
MARTY. … Flowers.

(Silence.)

MARTY. That was perfect.

(Blackout.)

III

They are all sitting in a circle.

LAUREN. Okay. Um.
    I was on the subway. In New York. And there was this old guy.
Who was … who was maybe Jewish.
    He had a beard.
    A-and …
    (A pause.)
    He was totally anti-Semitic.

(Lauren sighs.)

MARTY. It's okay, Lauren.
LAUREN. I don't remember anything else.

(Lauren sits back down.)

MARTY. Does anyone else remember something from the first day?

(A pause. No one says anything.)

MARTY. Okay. Well. I think maybe we'll do one more exercise
and then / call it a —

SCHULTZ. Wait! I do.

(Schultz stands up. He clears his throat.)

SCHULTZ. Uh … okay.
    I was at a wedding. In, ah … Eureka, California.
    Right near the Oregon border. Where there are a lot of red-
woods. It's really beautiful up there.
    This is nineteen-eighty … something.
    There was this big wedding. Two of my friends were getting

married in this big old hotel. And we … uh … we were all sleeping on straw mats. In the lobby. Of the hotel.

We were all drunk. And we'd been dancing.

And uh … there was this guy. I'd been looking at this guy all night. This really attractive, really beautiful guy who just … who caught my attention. But I didn't think anything would happen because he was just surrounded by women. All the women liked him.

(Pause.)

He was one of those guys. Those guys that get all the women.

(Pause.)

Then I was getting ready to go to sleep on my straw mat and I noticed that he was sitting … that he was lying next to me. On his straw mat. And even though they'd turned off all the lights I could tell that he was looking at me.

And I felt …

I felt seen.

And he smiled at me. I could feel him smiling in the dark.

And then I smiled back.

And neither of us had to say anything, because we knew that we would spend the / rest —

MARTY. Schultz?

SCHULTZ. — Of our lives together.

MARTY. That was great. Thank you.

SCHULTZ. I'm not finished.

MARTY. The thing is … it's quarter till, and I want to make sure we can squeeze in the last exercise.

SCHULTZ. … Oh. Okay.

(Silence.)

THERESA. That was beautiful, Schultz.

(Schultz can't quite bear to look at Theresa, but he nods.)

SCHULTZ. Yeah. Thanks.

(Blackout.)

IV

Schultz and Lauren stand in the center of the stage, facing each other. Marty, James, and Theresa watch.

SCHULTZ. *(To Marty.)*
  Five years?
MARTY. Ten years. Ten years from now.

(Schultz takes a deep breath.)

SCHULTZ. Okay.

(Schultz walks away from Lauren, then turns around and feigns surprise.)

SCHULTZ. Lauren?
LAUREN. Yeah?
SCHULTZ. Is that you?!
LAUREN. Yeah. Hi, Schultz.
SCHULTZ. Hey!

(Silence.)

SCHULTZ. What are you doing here in … Burlington?
LAUREN. Um … I live here now.
SCHULTZ. Weird. So do I!
  (Pause.)
  I live here with my wife.
LAUREN. You got married again?
SCHULTZ. Yeah. Yeah. She's fantastic.
LAUREN. That's so cool.
  (Pause.)
  What's her name?
SCHULTZ. Ah … Susan.
  Yeah.

She's a, uh …
She's a seamstress.
LAUREN. Wow.

(Silence.)

SCHULTZ. How are you?
LAUREN. I'm, um, I'm okay.
SCHULTZ. How old are you now?
LAUREN. I'm …
    (A pause while she calculates)
    … twenty-six.
SCHULTZ. Oh. Man. That's awesome.

(Silence.)

LAUREN. I live here with my boyfriend.
SCHULTZ. Aw. Great.
LAUREN. Todd.
SCHULTZ. That's great.
LAUREN. He's a, um … he's a doctor. Veterinarian.
    We run a veterinary clinic together.
SCHULTZ. What happened to acting?
LAUREN. Oh. Yeah.
SCHULTZ. I thought you wanted to be an actress.
LAUREN. No. I … I did a lot of acting in college. I was, like …
I starred in a lot of … but now I'm a veterinarian.
SCHULTZ. That's great.
LAUREN. I really like it.

(Silence.)

SCHULTZ. So you're happy?
LAUREN. Yeah. I think so.
SCHULTZ. Yeah.
LAUREN. Are you happy?
SCHULTZ. I am. I am. I'm very happy. Susan is just … she's
changed my life around. And business is going really well.
LAUREN. Are you still making your chairs?
SCHULTZ. Oh yeah. Oh yeah.

(Pause.)
Have you heard from any of the others?
LAUREN. Oh. Um —
SCHULTZ. Do you know how Theresa is doing?

(Marty opens her mouth and starts to step forward to interrupt them, but Theresa stops her.)

LAUREN. Um. Yeah.
(She glances over at Theresa.)
She's like a really successful massage therapist. In Putney.
SCHULTZ. Oh, that's good.
LAUREN. Yeah. And she married this, like, actor. He's kind of famous.

(Theresa giggles.)

LAUREN. I forget his name. He's really good-looking.
SCHULTZ. Huh. That's good.
(Pause.)
Man. She really screwed with my head.
LAUREN. ... Yeah.
SCHULTZ. But ah ... I don't really think about her that much anymore.
LAUREN. Yeah.
SCHULTZ. Have you heard from Marty or James?

(Marty shakes her head. Lauren thinks for a while.)

LAUREN. Um ... yeah. A couple of years ago. I got um ... I got like a Christmas card from Marty.
SCHULTZ. What'd she say?

(Over the next 30 seconds, the lights fade so that Marty, James, and Theresa eventually disappear, and only Lauren and Schultz remain, in a spotlight.)

LAUREN. Oh. She um. She moved to New Mexico.
SCHULTZ. Oh wow.
LAUREN. Yeah. She started some kind of like arts program? For

poor kids? Some kind of like drama thing?
SCHULTZ. Huh.
LAUREN. Yeah. She lives in Taos. In this really beautiful, um,
adobe hut. She sent me a picture.
SCHULTZ. So you two kept in touch.
LAUREN. Yeah. A little. I got ... it's funny. I didn't get the lead
in *West Side Story* that fall, but I got the um ... I got the part of
Anita? Which was actually —
SCHULTZ. Aw. I wish I'd known.
LAUREN. Yeah. I called Marty and told her. She came to see it.

(Silence. By this point, everything is different.)

SCHULTZ. So she and James aren't together anymore?

(Lauren shakes her head.)

SCHULTZ. Do you know where / he —
LAUREN. I think he's still in Shirley. At the college. Teaching
economics.
SCHULTZ. Huh.

(Silence.)

SCHULTZ. How's your family?
LAUREN. Oh. Um ... my parents got divorced this past fall.
    Yeah.
    After, um ... after thirty years of marriage.
SCHULTZ. I'm so sorry.
LAUREN. Yeah. No. I mean, I think it was a good decision.

(An awkward silence.)

LAUREN. Hey. Um. This is kind of a weird — but do you ever
wonder how many times your life is gonna end?

(Another silence.)

SCHULTZ. Uh ... I'm not sure I know what / you —
LAUREN. Like how many people you're ... like how many times

your life is gonna totally change and then, like, start all over again? And you'll feel like what happened before wasn't real and what's happening now is actually …

(She trails off.)

SCHULTZ. Uh … I don't know.

I guess I feel like my life is pretty real.

LAUREN. … Yeah.

(Silence.)

SCHULTZ. Well. Uh. It's great seeing you.

LAUREN. Yeah.

You too.

SCHULTZ. I always really liked you, Lauren.

LAUREN. Yeah. I liked you, too.

(They smile awkwardly at each other and do not move. Then, very faintly, we hear the sounds of a street in Burlington: people talking, a car honking, plates clinking at an outdoor restaurant.)

(The spotlight goes out.)

End of Play

PROPERTY LIST

Yoga ball
Bottles of water
3 cell phones
Hula hoop
Bags/backpacks
Nalgene water bottle
Wrapped sandwich
Flyer
5 pencils/pens
Wrapped box containing dreamcatcher